The Power of Love

PARTICIPANT'S GUIDE

TYNDALE HOUSE PUBLISHERS, INC.
Carol Stream, Illinois

Essentials of Parenting: The Power of Love
Participant's Guide

Copyright © 2011 by Focus on the Family
All rights reserved.

Focus on the Family and the accompanying logo and design are federally registered trademarks of Focus on the Family, Colorado Springs, CO 80995.

A Focus on the Family book published by Tyndale House Publishers, Carol Stream, Illinois 60188

TYNDALE is a registered trademark of Tyndale House Publishers, Inc. Tyndale's quill logo is a trademark of Tyndale House Publishers, Inc.

All Scripture quotations, unless otherwise indicated, are taken from the *Holy Bible, New International Version*®. NIV®. Copyright © 1973, 1978, 1984 by Biblica, Inc.™ Used by permission of Zondervan. All rights reserved worldwide. (www.zondervan.com).

No part of this publication may be reproduced, stored in a retrieval system, or transmitted in any form or by any means—electronic, mechanical, photocopy, recording, or otherwise—without prior permission of Focus on the Family.

Cover design by Ron Kaufman
Cover photograph copyright © Studio 1One/Shutterstock. All rights reserved.

ISBN: 978-1-58997-577-4

Printed in the United States of America
1 2 3 4 5 6 7 / 16 15 14 13 12 11

CONTENTS

Welcome! v

1 Not Just a Project 1

2 Depending on Dad 11

3 Mirrors and Buckets 23

4 The Two Faces of Love: Affirmation 35

5 The Two Faces of Love: Discipline 47

6 Preparing Your Heart to Parent 59

Notes 70

About Our DVD Presenters 71

QUICK START GUIDE FOR PARENTS

Whether you're studying in a group, as a couple, or individually, this book is for you. It's packed with discussion questions, advice, biblical input, and application activities.

But maybe all you'd like to do right now is watch the accompanying DVD and talk about it with your spouse—or think about it on your own. If so, go directly to the "Catching the Vision" section of each chapter. There you'll find the discussion questions you're looking for.

When you have more time, we encourage you to explore the other features in this book. We think you'll find them . . . essential!

WELCOME!

If there's anything you don't need, it's one more thing to do.

Unless, of course, that one thing might make the *other* things a whole lot easier.

We can't guarantee that this course will take all the challenge out of parenthood. It won't keep your kids from forgetting their lunch money, make them trade in their video games for art museum passes, or remind them to scoop the cat's litter box.

But it *will* help you understand why your parenting is so crucial, how to connect with your kids and encourage them to connect with their Creator, and how to enjoy the journey to the fullest. That's because you'll learn the essentials—what's vital to a healthy parent-child relationship, keys to protecting and training and affirming kids, and what God considers most important in bringing up boys and girls.

In other words, you'll discover how to be the mom or dad you really want to be.

That takes effort, but it doesn't take boredom or busywork. So we've designed this course to be provocative and practical. At its heart is an entertaining, down-to-earth video series featuring many of today's most popular parenting experts. And in your hands is the book that's going to make it all personal for you—the Participant's Guide.

In each chapter of this book, you'll find the following sections:

Finding Yourself. Take this survey to figure out where you stand on the subject at hand.

Catching the Vision. Use this section as you watch and think about the DVD.

Digging Deeper. This Bible study includes Scripture passages and thought-provoking questions.

Making It Work. Practice makes perfect, so here's your chance to begin applying principles from the DVD to your own family.

Bringing It Home. To wrap up, you'll find specific, encouraging advice you can use this week.

Whether you're using this book as part of a group or on your own, taking a few minutes to read and complete each chapter will bring the messages of the DVD home.

And isn't that exactly where you need it most?

Note: Many issues addressed in this series are difficult ones. Some parents may need to address them in greater detail and depth. The DVD presentations and this guide are intended as general advice only, and not to replace clinical counseling, medical treatment, legal counsel, or pastoral guidance.

Focus on the Family maintains a referral network of Christian counselors. For information, call 1-800-A-FAMILY and ask for the counseling department. You can also find plenty of parenting advice and encouragement at www.focusonthefamily.com.

Chapter 1

NOT JUST A PROJECT

Mel Brooks received a record 12 Tony Awards for his Broadway play *The Producers*. When asked about the key to his success, he answered, "You know, my feet never touched the floor until I was two because they were always passing me around and kissing and hugging me."

How will your kids describe your home when they grow up? Will they remember a dad who had a lucrative career and a low golf handicap, but who rarely spent significant time at home? If so, how will you feel when your grown son becomes a CEO and isn't much interested in his own kids, let alone spending time with you?

Most of us will readily admit that nothing in life—no *thing*—compares in importance to relationships. So why trade family for a boat, or seats on committees, or even the adulation of other church members for being "so involved"?

Maybe accomplishments, material possessions, or career positions seem crucial now. I promise you, though, that when you near the end of your life, you'll know that relationships matter most.

Why not recognize that truth today, while you still have time to do something about it?

—Dr. Kevin Leman[1]

2 THE POWER OF LOVE

FINDING YOURSELF

Identifying Your Needs

What role does relationship play in your parenting? What role would you like it to play? Here's a survey to get you thinking about that.

1. Which of the following would you most like your child to call you?
   - _X_ Mammi
   - _O_ Dady
   - ___ He (or She) Who Must Be Obeyed
   - ___ other _____

2. Which of the following do you think your child would like to be able to call you?
   - ___ friend
   - ___ total stranger
   - ___ billionaire philanthropist
   - _O_ other __Hero_____

3. If your childhood relationship with your parents were depicted in a movie, what might the title be?
   - _S_ *As Good as It Gets*
   - ___ *Monsters vs. Aliens*
   - ___ *Left Behind*
   - _O_ other _____

4. Which of the following parts of the parent-child relationship is most important to passing along your spiritual values?
   - _O_ listening
   - ___ forgiving

___ the part where you give everybody ice cream and silver dollars

___ other _____

5. The hardest part about maintaining a good relationship with your child is

   _0_ finding time to devote to it.

   ___ finding common ground in conversation.

   ___ finding his moldy fried mozzarella sticks on the couch for the thousandth time.

   ___ other _____

6. By the time you're done with this study, you hope to

   _0_ grow closer to your child.

   ___ grow closer to other parents who are going through the same things.

   ___ grow a spine and tell your child to get a job.

   ___ other _____

CATCHING THE VISION

Watching and Discussing the DVD

In this DVD segment, author Gary Thomas reminds us of a truth that many people miss: When it comes to parenting, it's all about the relationship.

Why? Because the alternative is seeing your child as a project, not a person. The focus turns to your child's behavior, performance, and development. That's not all bad, but it's not at the heart of what God calls us to do.

Project parenting leads moms and dads to become overly critical and fearful. *Will my child turn out right? Will he or she make a mistake, reflecting badly on me?*

God models something different. Everything He does for us, His children, is in the context of His loving relationship with us. Gary has some practical advice on how to follow God's lead.

After viewing the DVD, use questions like these to help you think through what you saw and heard.

1. How do you think the following would react to Gary's message? Why?
   - your parents
   - a child raised in an orphanage
   - you at the age of 12
   - your child

2. Which of the following parent-child relationships do you think Gary would be most pleased with? Why?
   - David and Solomon
   - Darth Vader and Luke Skywalker
   - Sanford and son
   - The von Trapps in *The Sound of Music*
   - Sheriff Taylor and Opie on *The Andy Griffith Show*

3. In which of the following situations would you be most tempted to treat your child as a project? Why?
   - Your 16-year-old son rarely washes his hair, and it looks really greasy.
   - Your 8-year-old daughter has perfect pitch, but won't practice the piano.
   - Your 3-year old son says only a few words and isn't potty-trained yet.

- Your 14-year-old daughter is such a tomboy that your mother keeps saying she's afraid the child might be gay.

4. How could relational parenting benefit you and your child in the following situations?
   - Your spouse is away in the military, deployed to the Middle East.
   - You think you're not good at teaching your child anything.
   - You think you're not good at relationships.
   - You and your child haven't gotten along well since he turned 13.

5. What's the difference between relationship parenting and friendship parenting? Which do you think is harder? Why? Which do you think your child would prefer? Why?

6. How might you use each of the following to help you improve your relationship with your child?
   - raking leaves
   - a dentist appointment
   - praying at bedtime
   - a three-day car trip

7. Which parent appearing in this DVD segment did you identify with most? Why?

8. Which of the following would you like to do with your child this week? How would you avoid treating him or her as a project while you're involved in the activity?
   - enter into her world by going to her favorite Web site together
   - draw pictures, take photos, paint, or sculpt clay
   - spend at least 10 minutes listening to him or her
   - memorize a Bible verse

DIGGING DEEPER

Bible Study

> *Jesus replied, "If anyone loves me, he will obey my teaching. My Father will love him, and we will come to him and make our home with him." (John 14:23)*

1. What kind of relationship is described here? How does it lead to godly behavior? How is it like—and unlike—the relationship a child has with a parent?

> *But as for you, continue in what you have learned and have become convinced of, because you know those from whom you learned it. (2 Timothy 3:14)*

2. What difference did it make that Timothy knew those from whom he'd learned the good news about Jesus? Would you rather learn about God from strangers or from people with whom you have a relationship? Why?

> *Therefore, although in Christ I could be bold and order you to do what you ought to do, yet I appeal to you on the basis of love. I then, as Paul—an old man and now also a prisoner of Christ Jesus—I appeal to you for my son Onesimus, who became my son while I was in chains. Formerly he was useless to you, but now he has become useful both to you and to me.*
>
> *I am sending him—who is my very heart—back to you. I would have liked to keep him with me so that he could take your place in helping me while I am in chains for the gospel. But I did not want to do anything without your consent, so that any favor you do will be spontaneous and not forced. Perhaps the reason he was separated from you for a little while was*

that you might have him back for good—no longer as a slave, but better than a slave, as a dear brother. He is very dear to me but even dearer to you, both as a man and as a brother in the Lord. (Philemon 8-16)

3. What kind of relationship did Paul have with Onesimus? With Philemon? How does Paul make the most of that relationship here? If you have any similar relationships, how might you use them to benefit everyone involved?

MAKING IT WORK

Applying the Principles

Here are some good ways to discover how to walk alongside your son or daughter, adapted from *Sticking with Your Teen* by Joe White with Lissa Halls Johnson (Focus on the Family/Tyndale, 2006). After each one, write a reply to the suggestion—using the key words listed. For example, one response to the first suggestion might be, "I'll let Brad choose what we do together next Saturday, and even if it's not my favorite thing, I won't just be a spectator."

1. *Find out what he loves to do.* Then do it *with* him, rather than just cheering him on from the stands. Key words: together, choose, spectator.
   Your reply:

2. *Make the most of summer.* Find a block of time *each* day when you can put your priorities, work, hobbies, and worries aside and be there 100 percent for your child. Key words: morning, evening, focus.
   Your reply:

3. *Take a wild adventure together.* One family hikes in the Rocky Mountains every year. Key words: exciting, tough, crazy.
   Your reply:

4. *Ask what your child has never done but would like to try.* Go try it together. Key words: new, risky, success.
   Your reply:

5. *Serve the needy together.* Homeless shelters, the Salvation Army, soup kitchens, food banks, convalescent homes, tutoring—the list of volunteer opportunities never gets shorter. Key words: month, need, give.
   Your reply:

6. *Find out what your child dreads doing.* Ask whether she wants your help with that PowerPoint project about bacteria or that awkward phone call to a friend whose sister just passed away. Key words: secret, fear, relieved.
   Your reply:

7. *Walk alongside your child spiritually.* Pray, read, and memorize Scripture with your child daily; just 10 minutes a day can give your relationship an "eternal touch." Key words: TV, talk, Bible.
   Your reply:

8. *Bring your child into your world.* When you run errands, invite one of your kids to come along. Key words: discover, spend, short.
   Your reply:

9. *Discover your child's dreams.* Help your child identify his strengths and work together toward realizing his dream. Key words: future, always, never.
   Your reply:

10. *Remember that the relationship is everything.* Earn a hearing by being the person your kids love hanging out with the most. Key words: listen, time, reward.

    Your reply:

BRINGING IT HOME

Insight for Your Week

Let me show you a tried and true method I use to get kids talking about what's bothering them. It's called active listening.

Begin by asking, "Would you like to talk about it now?"

If the answer is no, try again later.

When your child is open to talking, ask, "What's wrong?"

Listen to the answer. Then ask, "How do you feel?"

Listen some more. Then ask, "What are you doing about it?"

Listen again. Then ask, "What do you need to do?"

Listen further. Keep cycling through the questions as needed.

Let's see how this works in real life.

Your daughter comes home, sighs, drops her backpack on the floor, and slumps onto the couch.

"Do you feel like talking about it?" you ask.

"I guess," the girl mumbles.

"What's wrong?"

"Kerry told Shannon that I copied her test."

"How do you feel?"

"I'm totally angry at Kerry. She knows it's a lie. She knows I don't cheat."

"What are you doing about it?

"I don't know."

"What do you need to do?"

Your daughter shrugs and stares at the floor.

"What's wrong?" you ask again.

"I don't know if Kerry is my friend. I don't know why she'd say that."

"How do you feel about that?"

"Confused. Hurt."

"What are you doing about it?"

"I told Kaitlyn and Jo and Susan at lunch."

"What do you *need* to do?"

Your daughter sighs. "I probably need to talk to Kerry. I don't want to, though. I don't know what to say to her."

"How do you feel about confronting her?"

"Scared."

You get the idea. In a conversation like that, your child can let you in on the large and small traumas of her life, defusing their destructive power. It helps to have those exchanges as soon after the event as possible, but don't pressure your child to talk. And if you've avoided those conversations for so long that it seems awkward to bring up "old business," remember: "Better late than never."

—Joe White with Lissa Halls Johnson[2]

Chapter 2

DEPENDING ON DAD

A dad's primary, underlying job isn't control. It's to *validate* every one of his children.

To validate means to let your child know over and over and over, through words and actions, that the following are true:
- "Hey, you exist and you matter to me."
- "You're good enough."
- "You're an okay kid."

Psychotherapists sometimes talk about the *looking-glass-self principle*. It's the idea that children get their earliest, most lasting impressions of who they are from what's reflected back to them by their parents. These impressions become those "records" in the jukebox of your child's brain.

Let's say four-year-old Johnny walks into the room where his dad is reading the newspaper, and Dad doesn't confirm Johnny's presence. Dad doesn't say, "Good to see you, son!" He doesn't even say, "Don't bother me. Can't you see I'm trying to read?" Johnny may begin to doubt his own existence.

It's like the old, philosophical question: If a tree falls in the forest and there's nobody around to hear it, did it make a noise?

In Johnny's case, the answer is no. His existence hasn't been validated by any response. He interprets that to mean, *I'm not an okay person.* This may be a totally wrong interpretation; his dad may not believe this for a second about his son, but this is how Johnny—and most children—will interpret this scenario. That's the way children's brains operate.

A teenager needs as much of your time and attention as a toddler does. In fact, a dad's validation is so critical to a child's emotional health that he or she will go to any length—and I do mean any—to get it, whether it's real or artificial.

—Tim Sanford, Licensed Professional Counselor[3]

FINDING YOURSELF

Identifying Your Needs

The following questions can help you figure out where you stand on the subject of this session.

1. A father's most important parenting responsibility is
   ___ earning a living.
   ___ driving to church.
   ___ killing bugs.
   ___ other _____

2. Tenderness is to fathering as
   ___ feet are to slippers.
   ___ oil is to water.
   ___ mustard is to watermelon.
   ___ other _____

3. To "validate" your child means to
   ___ notice that he's alive and comment on it.
   ___ stamp his parking lot ticket.

___ take him to a psychology seminar where they use jargon like "validate."

___ other _____

4. If you learned anything from your own father, it was that

___ you could grow up to be president.

___ "the man" is out to get you.

___ automatic transmissions are for sissies.

___ other _____

5. The biggest difference between dads and moms is

___ anatomical.

___ emotional.

___ the way they shop for shoes.

___ other _____

6. The fatherhood role that means the most to you right now is

___ protecting and blessing your child.

___ representing authority.

___ yelling, "You call that racket 'music'?"

___ other _____

CATCHING THE VISION

Watching and Discussing the DVD

Being a dad is one of the most important jobs a man can have. It's also a daunting one: Reflect God's love and authority for your children, protect your family, and bless your kids with approval and validation.

What if your father didn't do these things for you perfectly—or at all? What if you don't feel up to the job?

Then you should join the club!

In this video segment, dads talk about the challenges and rewards of their roles. Carey Casey, CEO of the National Center for Fathering, tells how he's learned from research and experience to help fathers embrace their role and raise kids with sound values and fond memories that last. Dr. Bob Barnes, author of *Raising Confident Kids* (Zondervan, 1992) and executive director of Sheridan House Family Ministries, adds practical encouragement for dads, too.

After viewing the DVD, use questions like these to help you think through what you saw and heard.

1. Carey Casey is the author, with Neil Wilson, of a book called *Championship Fathering* (Focus on the Family/Tyndale, 2009). When you see that title, how do you feel? Which of the following comes closest to describing your reaction, and why?
    - "That's out of my (or my husband's) league."
    - "I (or my husband) can be a good dad without reading a book."
    - "That's the kind of father I want (or want my husband) to be."
    - other _____

2. Would your children call you (or your husband) an authority in your home? Why or why not? Do you want (or want your husband) to be seen that way? Why or why not?

3. In which of the following situations would you find it hardest to represent God's authority in your family? Why?
    - Your spouse calls you "spineless" in front of your children.
    - You feel guilty about having yelled at your kids last night when they were fighting at bedtime.
    - You just lost your house, and will have to move in with your parents.

- You're a new Christian, and aren't sure what kind of authority God is.

4. If God has given fathers an innate desire to protect and provide for their families, how would you explain the existence of the following? What happens when a father is physically or mentally unable to protect or provide?
    - "deadbeat dads"
    - police officers
    - child abuse
    - welfare

5. How could a father use each of the following to help his children feel more secure?
    - a cell phone
    - a dozen roses
    - a curfew
    - a song

6. In his book *Championship Fathering*, Carey writes as follows:

When I'm with a person who didn't have a good relationship with his father and who expresses some deep concern or need, I may pull him aside for a few minutes to talk. This is what I say. . . .

I was blessed to have a great dad. But I'm sure that if your dad could do it all over again, and he had the information and the opportunities that he needed, he would be different. There are things in place now that weren't in place then, so your dad didn't give you that. I'm not your dad, but let me say what I believe your dad would say if he were here: "*I'm proud of you.*"

Often, men will break down and cry right there—even football players whose arms are bigger than my legs.

Why do you think men have this reaction? What does it say about the importance of blessing your own children?

7. How would you bless your oldest child, using the following guidelines (one guideline per blessing)?
    - in 12 words or less
    - without using words at all
    - so that a three-year-old would understand what was going on

8. If you're a father, have you ever been mentored by another dad? If so, how did that work out? If not, why not? In which of the following areas would you be most interested in the help of another father?
    - loving
    - coaching
    - modeling
    - authority
    - protection
    - blessing

DIGGING DEEPER

Bible Study

Then I said to you, "Do not be terrified; do not be afraid of them. The LORD your God, who is going before you, will fight for you, as he did for you in Egypt, before your very eyes, and in the desert. There you saw how the LORD your God carried you, as a father carries his son, all the way you went until you reached this place." (Deuteronomy 1:29-31)

1. What role of a father is described here? How is the way an earthly father fulfills it different from the way God does? How is it similar?

> *"He is the one who will build a house for my Name, and I will establish the throne of his kingdom forever. I will be his father, and he will be my son. When he does wrong, I will punish him with the rod of men, with floggings inflicted by men. But my love will never be taken away from him, as I took it away from Saul, whom I removed from before you. Your house and your kingdom will endure forever before me; your throne will be established forever." (2 Samuel 7:13-16)*

2. In this passage, what does a father do? What's his attitude as he does it? Do you think most mothers perform the same function? Why or why not?

> *As a father has compassion on his children,*
> *so the LORD has compassion on those who fear him. (Psalm 103:13)*

3. Do you identify compassion more with fathers or mothers? Why? Do you think dads and moms express compassion in different ways? Why or why not?

> *My son, do not despise the LORD's discipline*
> *and do not resent his rebuke,*
> *because the LORD disciplines those he loves,*
> *as a father the son he delights in. (Proverbs 3:11-12)*

4. Would most parents in our culture see discipline as a sign of "delighting" in a child? Why or why not? Do you think dads would be more likely than moms to make this connection? Why or why not?

> *"Which of you fathers, if your son asks for a fish, will give him a snake instead? Or if he asks for an egg, will give him a scorpion? If you then, though you are evil, know how to give good gifts to your children, how much more will your Father in heaven give the Holy Spirit to those who ask him!" (Luke 11:11-13)*

5. What does this passage assume about fathers? If you're a father, what's the most recent "good gift" you gave your child?

> *Fathers, do not embitter your children, or they will become discouraged. (Colossians 3:21)*

6. Do you think fathers are more prone than mothers to "embitter" their kids? Why or why not? If you're a dad, what's one situation in which you especially need to remember this verse?

> *When Isaac was old and his eyes were so weak that he could no longer see, he called for Esau his older son and said to him, "My son."*
> *"Here I am," he answered.*
> *Isaac said, "I am now an old man and don't know the day of my death. Now then, get your weapons—your quiver and bow—and go out to the open country to hunt some wild game for me. Prepare me the kind of tasty food I like and bring it to me to eat, so that I may give you my blessing before I die." (Genesis 27:1-4)*

7. Why is it important for a father to bless his children? How is blessing like "validating"? If you're a dad, have you ever blessed your child? What happened?

MAKING IT WORK

Applying the Principles

One of the most important things a dad can do is listen. At a Father-Daughter Summit event sponsored by the National Center for Fathering, girls had plenty to say on the subject. Here are some of the things they said, adapted from *Championship Fathering*. After each statement, circle the word or phrase that best describes your response as a dad—or a mom.

1. "I wish my dad would try to understand what I'm going through, and be there when I need someone to talk to just as a friend and not as a parent."
   - I don't think I have a problem in this area.
   - I'll listen more carefully this week to better understand what my kids are going through.
   - other _____

2. "I need him to completely hear me out and not assume things . . . to listen before he speaks."
   - I don't think I have a problem in this area.
   - This week I'll make sure my kids get to speak their minds before I start talking.
   - other _____

3. "[I wish he] would take time and not talk but let me tell him one secret that I have hidden for a long time."
   - I don't think I have a problem in this area.
   - I'll try this week to earn my kids' trust so that they can tell me everything they want to.
   - other _____

4. "Try to see where I'm coming from before blowing up in my face and later wanting my forgiveness."
   - I don't think I have a problem in this area.
   - If I get angry at my child this week, I'll count to 10 (or more) before responding.
   - other _____

5. "Listen when I need you to. You don't have to have the right answers all the time; just be there for me."
   - I don't think I have a problem in this area.
   - When I don't know what to say to my child this week, I'll admit it.
   - other _____

6. "I wish my dad would just listen to me and not try to make everything about him."
   - I don't think I have a problem in this area.
   - When I talk with my kids this week, I'll consider their feelings before I think about my own.
   - other _____

7. "If my dad would listen and forgive me without always a punishment, I would open up and tell him more! I don't because I'm scared of getting grounded."
   - I don't think I have a problem in this area.
   - This week I'll cut in half the number of penalties I impose and see what happens.
   - other _____

8. "Actually stop and listen . . . don't think about what you're going to say, but hear and understand what I'm saying."
   - I don't think I have a problem in this area.
   - When I have a conversation with my child this week, I'll try not to compose my responses while he or she is talking.
   - other _____

9. "Listen to me [without trying] to fix the problem or discipline me for it, but just listen."
   - I don't think I have a problem in this area.

- This week I'll ask whether my child wants me to suggest a solution before I offer one.
- other _____

10. "Don't talk; don't argue; just listen."
    - I don't think I have a problem in this area.
    - Instead of arguing this week, I'll resist the urge to "win" and settle for really hearing what my child has to say.
    - other _____

BRINGING IT HOME

Insight for Your Week

Validating your child is like putting your stamp on his psyche. It tells him, "Yes, you are here at this moment."

Why is this such a big deal? Because most of us feel unaccepted, or at least invisible, until someone tells us otherwise.

I had to learn this lesson the hard way. Having been a serious football player and coach, a field that requires strict discipline and analyzing every replayed step, I had a problem with perfectionism. I've also had a critical spirit from day one. I didn't realize this until the day I criticized my son Brady—a sweet, gentle boy—and my wife Debbie Jo told me, "Joe, Brady sees himself in your eyes."

Her comment stopped me dead in my tracks. For Brady's first few years I'd been an absent dad; now I was an overly critical one. I'd been assessing my kids, not affirming them.

In time I learned to tell when I'd been overly critical with one of my kids. His countenance would fall, the head and eyes would lower, the body would sag. A parent who loves to be "large and in charge" might take that as a sign of victory; a parent who's looking for relationship knows it's a defeat for both of you.

I'm still fighting my critical, perfectionistic tendencies. But I've worked and prayed to validate my kids. To prove it, my tongue has a blister on it where I've bitten it so many times!

So how can you validate your son or daughter?

It can be as simple as acknowledging that your child is in the room. Or saying hello to her when you get home from work. Or using her name when you speak with her.

Or you can get more creative. Validating a 16-year-old son might mean tossing him the family car keys for the evening. For a 15-year-old daughter who likes to cook, it might mean trusting her to choose the menu when your boss comes for dinner.

Ask about your child's dreams and encourage them. Look at his charcoal drawings; listen to her homegrown band that's been whanging away in the garage.

Find out what music he's listening to, and listen to it yourself—not just to monitor it, but so that you can discuss it intelligently with him. If she's involved in sports, help coach the team. Or at least practice with her, finding out about swim strokes and what makes one stronger and more efficient than another. Go to every game or meet or recital you can. Follow up with positive comments that show you were paying attention.

Don't just applaud performance, though; you're validating the person, not the talent. Focus on character, speaking up when you see inner strength. One father says things like, "I saw you give your last dollar to that lady, Son. You have such a generous spirit." Or, "I'm proud of you for making the right decision about helping your sister with her homework."

A lot of kids are starving for that kind of attention. One young man, living in a home for troubled teens, said, "I have never once heard my parents say, 'I'm proud of you.' It's always been, 'You're a smart kid, but. . . . ' 'You're a good-lookin' kid, but. . . .'" As that boy told us his story, you could feel his ache to be validated filling the room.

—Joe White with Lissa Halls Johnson[4]

Chapter 3

MIRRORS AND BUCKETS

What about a mom's primary job? It's not cooking dinner, changing diapers, or helping a preschooler glue colored macaroni on a coffee can as a Father's Day gift.

The most important assignment a mom has is to *nurture* her children.

But what does that mean, exactly? Most of us have a vague notion about what being nurtured feels like, but here are a few specifics. A nurturing mom goes beyond being the "maintenance person" in a child's life. She doesn't just keep a child clean, fed, warm, and dry. She also helps enable her children to develop fully by pouring life into them. She models joy and passion. Nurturing is filling your child up with aliveness.

It's not a joyless, self-sacrificing caricature of Betty Crocker. A nurturing mom takes time to play, read, and take pictures when the toddler's spaghetti ends up on the head instead of in the mouth. She enters the child's world to see things from his or her perspective, even if it means the carpets don't get vacuumed for a while. She provides empathetic understanding from a position of strength and support. That's true whether she's dealing with a toddler or a teen—except for the part about spaghetti on the head.

Before you feel burdened with a mile-long list you can never follow through on, let me be quick to say that nurturing is not about "doing it all" or doing it perfectly. It's about doing the best you can—without losing yourself or driving yourself crazy because your own needs aren't taken care of. You won't be able to nurture your children if you're exhausted from burning the candle at both ends.

So please take care of yourself, too. *You* need aliveness in order to pass it on to your kids.

—Tim Sanford, Licensed Professional Counselor[5]

FINDING YOURSELF

Identifying Your Needs

Take a couple of minutes to fill out the following survey.

1. Most mothers should be
    ___ put on a pedestal.
    ___ committed to a mental institution.
    ___ compensated for their parental duties at the same rate as fathers.
    ___ other _____

2. When it comes to nurturing, your role model is
    ___ your own mother.
    ___ Mother Teresa.
    ___ Mother Goose.
    ___ other _____

3. The main task of motherhood is
    ___ preparing a child's heart for a relationship with God.
    ___ preparing a child's heart for relationships with others.
    ___ preparing dinner.
    ___ other _____

4. Moms are typically better than dads at
   ___ expressing feelings.
   ___ spelling.
   ___ claiming to be better than the opposite sex at certain things.
   ___ other _____

5. The hardest part of being a mom is
   ___ "mommy guilt."
   ___ stretch marks.
   ___ putting up with a dad.
   ___ other _____

6. God is like a mother in the sense that He
   ___ wants to gather His people as a hen gathers chicks (Matthew 23:37).
   ___ comforts His children as a mother comforts hers (Isaiah 66:13).
   ___ is omnipresent, all-seeing, and all-knowing (Psalm 139).
   ___ other _____

CATCHING THE VISION

Watching and Discussing the DVD

Mothers have a big job to do—several of them, in fact. Focus on the Family psychologist and broadcast host Dr. Juli Slattery believes moms are meant to be teachers, among other things. Their subjects include managing emotions, connecting with other people, and separating from Mom herself.

In this DVD segment, Juli uses some colorful comparisons to help parents understand the roles of mothers. Get ready to hear about mirrors and buckets, for example. Since Juli is an experienced mom as well as counselor and author, you'll hear how she's handled things, too. As she's said before, "We want to do it perfectly, but we know we mess up. The awesome thing is that through my failures and limitations as a mom, I can teach my kids about God's perfection. You don't have to be a perfect mom; just be a faithful one."

After viewing the DVD, use questions like these to help you think through what you saw and heard.

1. What are three things you've taught your oldest child? If you're a mom, how did you do it? If you're a dad, how did you do it? Do you think mothers and fathers teach differently? Why or why not?

2. If you're a mom, how would you feel if you heard the following from your child? If you're a dad, how would you expect your wife to feel?
   - "My stomach hurts."
   - "You never make macaroni anymore."
   - "I hate you."
   - "The kids at school think I'm ugly."

3. Which of the following are examples of being a "mirror"? Which are examples of being a "bucket"? Why?
   - Saying to your child, "You're shouting. Please use your inside voice."
   - Telling your child, "We'll find your doll. Let's stop for a second and ask God to help us."
   - Explaining to your child, "Grandpa is in heaven now. His body is still here, but it's like a tent that he doesn't have to live in anymore."
   - Saying to your child, "I think you miss your friend Sarah since she moved away. If you'd like to call her, go ahead."

4. Who acts as a mirror to you? Who is your most faithful "bucket"? What have you learned from that person that you could apply to your relationship with your child?

5. Juli describes motherhood as an emotionally intense experience. How would you compare it to the following in terms of emotional intensity? Why?
   - being a father
   - going to Disney World
   - surviving an earthquake
   - doing a tour of duty in a war zone

6. What would you do in each of the following situations to teach your child about connecting with other people? Do you think moms are better equipped than dads to do this? Why or why not?
   - Your shy 6-year-old is invited to a birthday party and doesn't want to go.
   - Your 8-year-old is suspended from school for bullying.
   - Your 10-year-old feels betrayed by a friend who's started sitting with someone else at lunch.
   - Your 14-year-old seems to spend five hours a day sending messages via texting, Facebook, and Twitter.

7. Moms often feel pressure to be perfect. Which of the following do you think are required by God, and which are required mainly by family members, acquaintances, or mothers themselves?
   - cooking dinner every night
   - knowing how to sew
   - never being angry with your child
   - making sure your child has enough friends
   - leading your child to become a Christian

8. Which of these word pictures seems to best describe you (or your wife, if you're a dad)? Why?
    - gas station
    - safe base
    - flight instructor
    - other _____

DIGGING DEEPER

Bible Study

"Can a mother forget the baby at her breast
and have no compassion on the child she has borne?
Though she may forget,
I will not forget you!" (Isaiah 49:15)

1. What does this passage assume about mothers? Would you say that most moms can't help but feel compassion for their children? Why or why not?

"As a mother comforts her child,
so will I comfort you;
and you will be comforted over Jerusalem."
(Isaiah 66:13)

2. Do you think most children turn to mothers or fathers first for comfort? Does it work that way in your family? Why or why not?

As apostles of Christ we could have been a burden to you, but we were gentle among you, like a mother caring for her little children. (1 Thessalonians 2:6-7)

3. In your experience, does gentleness seem to come more naturally to moms than to dads? If you're a mom, how would you express gentleness in the following situations?

   ___ Your 3-year-old sits on a juice box—on your favorite chair.
   ___ Your 6-year-old needs eyedrops for an infection—and closes his eyes every time you try to get them in.
   ___ Your 13-year-old shows up for dinner with three hungry friends—and without warning.

*Listen, my son, to your father's instruction
and do not forsake your mother's teaching. (Proverbs 1:8)*

4. Are there certain subjects that you think mothers can teach their children better than fathers can? If so, what are they? What's one thing you learned from your mother that you'd like to pass on to your kids?

*A wife of noble character who can find?
She is worth far more than rubies. . . .
She selects wool and flax
and works with eager hands.
She is like the merchant ships,
bringing her food from afar.
She gets up while it is still dark;
she provides food for her family
and portions for her servant girls.
She considers a field and buys it;
out of her earnings she plants a vineyard.
She sets about her work vigorously;
her arms are strong for her tasks.
She sees that her trading is profitable,
and her lamp does not go out at night.
In her hand she holds the distaff
and grasps the spindle with her fingers.*

*She opens her arms to the poor
and extends her hands to the needy.
When it snows, she has no fear for her household;
for all of them are clothed in scarlet.
She makes coverings for her bed;
she is clothed in fine linen and purple. . . .
She makes linen garments and sells them,
and supplies the merchants with sashes.
She is clothed with strength and dignity;
she can laugh at the days to come.
She speaks with wisdom,
and faithful instruction is on her tongue.
She watches over the affairs of her household
and does not eat the bread of idleness.
Her children arise and call her blessed;
her husband also, and he praises her:
"Many women do noble things,
but you surpass them all." (Proverbs 31:10, 13-22, 24-29)*

5. Of all the qualities and activities listed in this passage, which three do you think are most important for a mother to be and do? Of those three, which one is most important to your children right now?

MAKING IT WORK

Applying the Principles

How prepared are you to handle the job of motherhood? Here's one way to find out. Whether you're a mom, a dad, or just hope to be one of those someday, try filling out the following employment application, based on Proverbs 31. Then choose three areas in which you'd like to "upgrade your skills" during the next month.

APPLICATION FOR EMPLOYMENT
Position: Proverbs 31 Woman, Grade 7

Please summarize briefly your experience in each of the following areas. Preference will be given to candidates whose experience has been gained in a parental setting.

1. Displays noble character _____
2. Works with eager hands _____
3. Brings food from afar _____
4. Gets up early _____
5. Makes wise investments _____
6. Has strong arms _____
7. Makes profitable trades _____
8. Works late _____
9. Has domestic skills _____
10. Helps the poor _____
11. Prepares family for bad weather _____
12. Makes things the family needs _____
13. Earns money _____
14. Has strength and dignity _____
15. Doesn't worry over the future _____
16. Speaks wisely _____
17. Gives faithful instruction _____
18. Manages the household _____
19. Avoids idleness _____
20. Earns praise from the family _____

BRINGING IT HOME

Insight for Your Week

Validating says you exist. Nurturing says, "Not only do you exist, but I'm going to do what I can to help your heart and spirit thrive."

There's a tenderness to nurturing. I happen to believe that God has given moms especially tender hearts, which suits them perfectly to this job.

Nurturing, like validation, comes in many forms. Here are three big ones: touch, words, and actions.

1. *Nurturing touch.* Much has been said about how we fail to thrive when nobody touches us. A daily hug is a great place to start. But when you're a teenager, it's not cool to want a hug from your mom. So some moms have declared that *they* need a hug every day. By making it *your* need, you take the pressure off.

Other forms of touch are less intrusive, but still provide nurturing. Try the brush of a hand across an arm, or a pat on the back. Plant a kiss on the cheek or the top of the head while your student is studying or watching television. Daughters often love having their hair braided while the two of you take in a movie on the small screen; one mother said her girls would flop on the sofa and fling their hair onto her lap for her to fiddle with. Sons, meanwhile, will sometimes let their moms massage their heads while viewing TV. Be creative as well as appropriate.

2. *Nurturing words.* "Sticks and stones may break my bones, but words will never hurt me." The sad truth is that hurtful words go much deeper than a bruise or a broken bone.

Like the rest of us, kids collect negative words and play them back subconsciously:

"You're stupid and ugly and no one will ever want you."

"You can't do anything right."

"Go away. You're being a nuisance."

"You're just like all the other kids—selfish."

"Come on! Think!"

Have you heard yourself utter words you wish you could take back? Try words like these that soothe, build up, and encourage:

"I'm so proud you're my daughter."

"Man! You look fabulous today."

"Do you know how much I love you?"

"Want to go shopping with me? I really enjoy your company."

There are so many chances to nuture your child verbally. You hold the key in your words and tone of voice.

3. *Nurturing actions.* Here's what one teen who feels nurtured by her mom has to say:

"When I'm going through a tough time, it helps me to cry to my mom. She sits there and gives me a shoulder to cry on and lets me say everything I need to get out. Just knowing she is there to help me out helps me get through tough times. When I finish crying, we talk through what I/we can do to improve/fix the situation."

That mom knows nurturing isn't all talk and touch. Sometimes it's listening.

Sometimes it's doing other things for your child. For example:
- If it's time to study for finals, bring her hot chocolate or cookies or cut-up fruit in a bowl.
- Do his chores for a day when he's having a bad one.
- Stick you-can-do-it notes on the mirror in her bathroom or bedroom.
- Tuck greeting cards inside his notebook or textbook.
- Text-message a hello.

—Joe White with Lissa Halls Johnson[6]

Chapter 4

THE TWO FACES OF LOVE: AFFIRMATION

Nicolas Copernicus' idea was simple, but revolutionary: The sun, not the Earth, lies at the center of our solar system.

Today, no thinking person would dispute this. But at the time, Copernicus' idea rocked the world scientifically and theologically. People had assumed that everything revolved around the Earth, a view that seemed to fit the scientific data as well as religious beliefs of the day. Humans were, of course, at the center of it all.

Many parents today live under a similar illusion. They think that believing in your child means making him the center of your family.

That may seem at first the noble and loving thing to do. But making your child the family's center—perhaps putting your relationship with your spouse on hold for 18 years—spells trouble.

A *family-centered child* rather than a *child-centered family* produces a more giving person. If you're a family with a faith and everything centers around giving your child Disneyland on Earth, will he or she understand the need for God? That child is likely to develop sky-high expectations—namely, that his well-being is primary and all else is secondary. If your aim is to raise a child who'll look out for others before himself, you've missed the mark.

You want to communicate that you're there for your child. You don't want to go too far and communicate that you're there *only* for your child.

—Dr. Kevin Leman[7]

FINDING YOURSELF

Identifying Your Needs

How do you feel about balancing love and limits—affirmation and discipline? Take this survey to express yourself.

1. Which of the following do you think a child could live without?
    - ___ affirmation
    - ___ discipline
    - ___ high-speed Internet access
    - ___ other _____

2. When you were growing up, your family emphasized
    - ___ love over limits.
    - ___ limits over love.
    - ___ carbs over calories.
    - ___ other _____

3. Affirming your child is better than inflating her self-esteem because
    - ___ the former sounds healthier.
    - ___ the former is cheaper.
    - ___ the latter could lead her to run for office.
    - ___ other _____

4. People who know you well would describe your approach to discipline as
    - ___ authoritative.
    - ___ permissive.
    - ___ probably illegal.
    - ___ other _____

5. Healthy affirmation consists of
   ___ affiliation, acceptance, and affection.
   ___ flattery, flowers, and fried foods.
   ___ cards, candy, and cash.
   ___ other _____

6. Which of the following would you agree with?
   ___ Children should be accepted for who they are and encouraged for what they do.
   ___ Children should be measured by their performance and corrected for their failures.
   ___ Children should be seen and not heard, except when playing a musical instrument.
   ___ other _____

CATCHING THE VISION

Watching and Discussing the DVD

How do you show your children you love them? Mainly through affirmation and discipline. Contrary to some conventional wisdom, those two don't conflict; they complement each other.

In this DVD segment, author and speaker Julie Barnhill—along with Dr. Bob Barnes, author, radio host, and executive director of Sheridan House Family Ministries—address the first part of the love equation. Affirmation, they indicate, isn't the same as ego inflation. Nor is it a way to manipulate kids into performing. It's a clear message of unconditional love, the same message God has sent us.

But what if your kids aren't doing what you want them to? What's the difference between acceptance and approval? And how can you help your children feel valued not only as individuals but as family members? Julie and Bob have plenty to say about those issues, too, in this practical presentation.

After viewing the DVD, use questions like these to help you think through what you saw and heard.

1. If you needed an expert to come to your home and show you how to affirm your kids, would you choose Julie or Bob? Why?

2. When you hear the word "affirmation," which of the following come to mind?
    - undeserved praise
    - high fives
    - the word "yes"
    - other _____

3. How could understanding the difference between approval and acceptance help in each of the following situations?
    - Your child doesn't want to go to church anymore.
    - You wish your child would lose weight.
    - Your child isn't interested in carrying on the family business someday.
    - You know your child could get better grades if she tried, but she won't.

4. Since children are a reflection of us, parents who feel embarrassed or disappointed by them may be tempted to deal with them harshly. If you could raise your kids anonymously—that is, without anyone knowing they're yours—would you do so? Why or why not?

5. When it comes to affirming your child, how would you rank the following from most effective to least effective? If you could add one more, what would it be?
    - positive words
    - appropriate physical touch
    - eye contact
    - one-on-one time
    - listening
    - inviting him or her into your world

6. Part of affirming children is letting them know they're valued members of a family. When it comes to being a team, which of the following best describes your household? How do you feel about that?
    - the Chicago Cubs
    - the United Nations Security Council
    - Ringling Bros. and Barnum & Bailey Circus
    - the heavenly host
    - the X-Men
    - other _____

7. Which of the following principles have you seen proven in your household? How?
    - Feeling like part of a family gives a child confidence.
    - Contributing to a family prepares a child for work, marriage, and church.
    - Chores are a basic way to build a team mentality.
    - Being part of a family should help you feel safe, accepted, and energized.

8. After watching this DVD segment, has your definition of "affirmation" changed? Why or why not?

DIGGING DEEPER

Bible Study

In each of the following passages, what percentage would you say is about affirmation? How much is about discipline? In 12 words or less, how would you paraphrase each passage in a way that would help your child understand how affirmation and discipline go together?

You were shown these things so that you might know that the LORD is God; besides him there is no other. From heaven he made you hear his voice to discipline you. On earth he showed you his great fire, and you heard his words from out of the fire. Because he loved your forefathers and chose their descendants after them, he brought you out of Egypt by his Presence and his great strength, to drive out before you nations greater and stronger than you and to bring you into their land to give it to you for your inheritance, as it is today. (Deuteronomy 4:35-38)

Affirmation %:
Discipline %:
Paraphrase:

*He who spares the rod hates his son,
but he who loves him is careful to discipline him. (Proverbs 13:24)*

Affirmation %:
Discipline %:
Paraphrase:

Those whom I love I rebuke and discipline. So be earnest, and repent. Here I am! I stand at the door and knock. If anyone hears my voice and opens the door, I will come in and eat with him, and he with me. (Revelation 3:19-20)

Affirmation %:
Discipline %:
Paraphrase:

In your struggle against sin, you have not yet resisted to the point of shedding your blood. And you have forgotten that word of encouragement that addresses you as sons:

"My son, do not make light of the Lord's discipline,
and do not lose heart when he rebukes you,
because the Lord disciplines those he loves,
and he punishes everyone he accepts as a son."

Endure hardship as discipline; God is treating you as sons. For what son is not disciplined by his father? If you are not disciplined (and everyone undergoes discipline), then you are illegitimate children and not true sons. Moreover, we have all had human fathers who disciplined us and we respected them for it. How much more should we submit to the Father of our spirits and live! Our fathers disciplined us for a little while as they thought best; but God disciplines us for our good, that we may share in his holiness. No discipline seems pleasant at the time, but painful. Later on, however, it produces a harvest of righteousness and peace for those who have been trained by it. (Hebrews 12:4-11)

Affirmation %:
Discipline %:
Paraphrase:

"I am with you and will save you,"
declares the LORD.
"Though I completely destroy all the nations
among which I scatter you,
I will not completely destroy you.
I will discipline you but only with justice;
I will not let you go entirely unpunished." (Jeremiah 30:11)

Affirmation %:
Discipline %:
Paraphrase:

42 THE POWER OF LOVE

MAKING IT WORK

Applying the Principles

Here's a map. Drawing a line, show how you'd get from "Start" to "Finish." The catch: Draw your route only through places that represent *healthy* affirmation or discipline. Avoid *unhealthy* places. That means, of course, you'll have to decide which are which!

START

- Negotiating Curfew with a 16-Year-Old
- Washing Mouth Out with Soap
- Spanking in Anger
- Thanking Child for Feeding the Dog
- Promising Child Candy for Going to Church
- Yelling at Child for Eating a Cookie Before Dinner
- Negotiating Bedtime with a 6-Year-Old
- Throwing a Party for a C-Average Report Card
- Forgiving Child for Saying "I Hate You"
- Apologizing for Yelling at Child
- Saying "That's a Nice Shirt You're Wearing"
- Yelling at Child for Shoplifting
- Time-Out for Biting Younger Sister
- Saying "You Never Think of Anyone Else"
- Time-Out for Hitting Older Brother
- Losing Allowance for a Month over Cheating on Test

FINISH

Questions to think about:
How did you decide what was healthy or unhealthy?

When it comes to affirmation and discipline, how can you remember to stick with healthy places and avoid unhealthy ones this week?

BRINGING IT HOME

Insight for Your Week

Children who grow up in legalistic, strict environments in which the parents never explain the purpose of discipline will often obey just as long as Mom and Dad are watching, then act up the second their parents turn their heads. On the other hand, kids who grow up in homes that lack rules and standards, where the parents are buddies rather than authority figures, often know the right thing to do but don't have the willpower to carry it out.

It takes time and energy to teach our kids why they're being corrected, rather than to simply dole out the punishment. For example, if Clancy interrupts me while I'm talking on the phone, the most convenient thing for me to do is to send her to her room. This stops her negative behavior and allows me to continue my conversation with only a brief pause in my personal agenda. But it's not the best approach, because all Clancy has learned is that this time she got caught. The next time she has a burning question, she'll probably interrupt me again.

I'm not saying we shouldn't send children to their rooms. But discipline alone isn't enough; we must follow up. So after I send Clancy to her room, I should cut my conversation a little short and then join her upstairs. That way I can explain to her why interrupting is inconsiderate—both to me and to the other person on the line. I can relay that when she interrupts me, she is communicating a selfish message: that what she has to say is more important than what I or anyone else has to say. This gives me the opportunity to talk to Clancy about putting others first.

Of course, we as parents should be sensitive to our kids, too. Often the question is important! So at our house, we use a wonderful technique, called the "Interrupt Rule," that we learned in a parenting class. Using this technique, our kids will gently rest a hand on my side when they need to get my attention. I'll lay my hand on theirs, acknowledging the request to speak, and then at a logical break in my conversation, I'll excuse myself and briefly turn my attention to my child.

It takes time to follow up our discipline by explaining the rules and then describing what to do in the future. But it's worth it! We'll be raising children who do the right things for the right reasons.

The goal is for our kids to make obedient choices because they know it's the right thing to do, because it pleases God—not because they want to avoid correction. If our children are motivated to obey only out of fear, they'll miss the whole point of obedience.

I must confess that if I'd been able to force my children to obey me out of fear while they were young, I would have parented that way. It's so much easier—but it's the wrong approach. In hindsight, I'm glad I was unsuccessful at using fear tactics. It would have made life simpler while my kids were young, but I'd rather see them obey me—and God—wholeheartedly, out of love.

Of course, there's always the temptation to let the pendulum swing too far to the other side. That approach is dangerous, though, for our kids need correction. It isn't enough to give only information and unconditional love in the hope that they will eventually make the right choices.

I have to confess again that I have given this technique my best shot, too. I've been known to give my children an overdose of information when a little bit of correction would have been more effective. In fact, I did it as recently as last week. I had just delivered lecture number 286, addressing an aspect of Tucker's behavior that needed improving, when he made a comment that made me cringe.

"You know, Mom," Tucker said seriously after listening to me drone on, "you should put all these sermons on a tape so I can play them when I go to bed. That way, they'd get into my heart all night—and if I'm having trouble settling down, they can help put me to sleep!" (Tucker didn't mean any disrespect—I really am that verbose sometimes. Please pray for me.)

We can talk our children to death. If we do not discipline them when they're young, they will have a difficult time disciplining themselves when they're older.

—Lisa Whelchel[8]

Chapter 5

THE TWO FACES OF LOVE: DISCIPLINE

Several years ago, Steve and I attended a five-day seminar in Chicago. Before we left, we farmed out our children, ages two, three, and four, to various friends' houses. Each child had a fabulous time with his or her buddies, but all three were glad when Mommy and Daddy returned. The reunion, however, was short-lived: Steve and I had to attend a meeting at church the very night we arrived home.

I realized the kids had probably gotten away with "who knows what" while we were gone and that they'd be frustrated we were leaving again. I was especially worried about the baby-sitter. Would she be able to handle them?

In an effort to work "damage control," I warned Tucker, "I really want you to do your best to obey the baby-sitter tonight."

"Well, Mom, I just don't know if I can do that," he admitted.

My eyebrows rose. "Why?"

With a straight face, Tucker said, "There's so much foolishness built up in my heart, I don't think there is any room for goodness and wisdom."

"Then maybe we need to step into the bathroom and drive that foolishness out," I suggested.

Tucker's eyes widened. "W-wait a minute," he sputtered. "I feel the foolishness going away all by itself—the goodness is coming in right now!"

I didn't know whether to laugh or cry.

—Lisa Whelchel[9]

FINDING YOURSELF

Identifying Your Needs

1. The word *discipline* comes from the word
   ___ *discipleship.*
   ___ *disc.*
   ___ *antidisestablishmentarianism.*
   ___ other _____

2. The real purpose of discipline is
   ___ to control a child's behavior.
   ___ to teach a child self-control.
   ___ to exercise your screaming muscles.
   ___ other _____

3. Spanking is
   ___ the first resort.
   ___ a last resort.
   ___ what you do when your child misbehaves in the lobby of an expensive resort.
   ___ other _____

4. God has disciplined you by
   ___ making you wander in the wilderness for 40 years.
   ___ giving you boils and killing your oxen.
   ___ letting somebody else get the best parking space at the mall.
   ___ other _____

5. The last time you disciplined your child,
   ___ he thanked you for it.

___ he didn't seem to notice.
___ he speed-dialed his attorney.
___ other _____

6. Your most pressing question about discipline is
   ___ "How can I get my child to obey?"
   ___ "Is corporal punishment okay?"
   ___ "Is it normal for kids to lock their parents in the closet like this?"
   ___ other _____

CATCHING THE VISION

Watching and Discussing the DVD

In this DVD segment, Julie Ann Barnhill and Dr. Bob Barnes return to discuss the "other side" of parental love: discipline. It's a widely misunderstood topic, often confused with punishment. Discipline is related to discipling; it's about teaching, not just behavior control.

Parents who discipline lovingly and effectively set the table for a healthy bond. The rest invite an adversarial relationship. Without clear boundaries, kids can't be sure whether "no means no" and often end up in a perpetual argument. And they fail to learn discipline's most important lesson: self-discipline.

Disciplining children may seem to risk damaging the parent-child relationship. But in the long run, you're building a stronger connection.

After viewing the DVD, use questions like these to help you think through what you saw and heard.

1. If you had to summarize the message of this video segment by drawing a picture, what would be in it?

2. If you changed "I need to *discipline* this child" to "I need to *disciple* this child," what might be your next step in each of the following situations?
    - Your 4-year-old son is pulling his 2-year-old sister's hair.
    - Your 15-year-old daughter posts a picture of herself in a bikini on the Internet.
    - Your 9-year-old son steals money from your dresser, then lies about it.
    - Your 3-year-old daughter won't stop singing the same VeggieTales song over and over.

3. What's one boundary you've been glad your family has set? Does your child share your enthusiasm? If not, do you still agree that effective, loving discipline is good for parent-child relationships over the long term? Why or why not?

4. If you had watched this video segment one year ago, might any of the events of the last year have been different? Why or why not?

5. What's your reaction to each of the following statements?
    - Discipline can be difficult for moms because they are typically the ones dealing with the day-to-day.
    - Getting mad isn't hard for moms, but well-thought-out, proactive decisions about discipline are difficult; they don't think about it in the heat of the moment.
    - Yelling is the new spanking.

6. What percentage of the responsibility for developing a child's self-discipline belongs with parents? What percentage lies with the child? What percentage belongs to God?

7. If the following were in charge of discipline in your house, how might it be different? Would you put any of the following in that position? Why or why not?
    - your mother
    - the Australian Army
    - the judges from *American Idol*
    - your oldest child

8. Which of the following are you most prepared to do this week? What further preparation might you need?
    - Have a family meeting to talk about discipline.
    - Tell your children, "My no means no."
    - Think through behaviors and consequences.
    - Have your resolve tested by your kids.

DIGGING DEEPER

Bible Study

The proverbs of Solomon son of David, king of Israel:
for attaining wisdom and discipline;
for understanding words of insight;
for acquiring a disciplined and prudent life,
doing what is right and just and fair. (Proverbs 1:1-3)

1. Do you think most people believe self-discipline is something you're born with, or that you can acquire? What does this passage have to say on that subject?

At the end of your life you will groan,
when your flesh and body are spent.

> *You will say, "How I hated discipline!*
> *How my heart spurned correction!*
> *I would not obey my teachers*
> *or listen to my instructors.*
> *I have come to the brink of utter ruin*
> *in the midst of the whole assembly." (Proverbs 5:11-14)*

2. How does your child respond when you warn of what might happen someday if he or she doesn't use sunscreen, turn down the volume of an MP3 player, or turn homework in on time? How might he or she respond to Proverbs 5:11-14?

> *Whoever loves discipline loves knowledge,*
> *but he who hates correction is stupid. (Proverbs 12:1)*

3. On a scale of 1 to 10 (10 highest), how much does your child love discipline? How much does he or she hate correction? Have you found any good ways to correct your child without being too harsh or discouraging?

> *"I have surely heard Ephraim's moaning:*
> *'You disciplined me like an unruly calf,*
> *and I have been disciplined.*
> *Restore me, and I will return,*
> *because you are the* LORD *my God.*
> *After I strayed,*
> *I repented;*
> *after I came to understand,*
> *I beat my breast.*
> *I was ashamed and humiliated*
> *because I bore the disgrace of my youth.'*

*Is not Ephraim my dear son,
the child in whom I delight?
Though I often speak against him,
I still remember him.
Therefore my heart yearns for him;
I have great compassion for him,"
declares the* LORD. *(Jeremiah 31:18-20)*

4. How can you tell that discipline is helping Ephraim develop self-discipline? In the last year, have you seen evidence that your child is doing the same? If so, what is it?

   For God did not give us a spirit of timidity, but a spirit of power, of love and of self-discipline. (2 Timothy 1:7)

5. If God has given us a spirit of self-discipline, why do parents need to discipline their kids? What do you think would happen if you left the job entirely up to God?

   So then, let us not be like others, who are asleep, but let us be alert and self-controlled. For those who sleep, sleep at night, and those who get drunk, get drunk at night. But since we belong to the day, let us be self-controlled, putting on faith and love as a breastplate, and the hope of salvation as a helmet. (1 Thessalonians 5:6-8)

6. When it comes to self-control, would you describe your child as sleepwalking, groggy, or alert in the following areas? What kind of "wake-up call" might help?
   ___ learning to manage money
   ___ exercising and eating a healthy diet
   ___ telling the truth

MAKING IT WORK

Applying the Principles

Discipline is all about working yourself out of a job—by helping your child learn *self*-discipline. But what kinds of self-discipline does your child especially need to learn?

Here are three situations in which your child would benefit from exercising self-discipline. If you could choose your own ending to each story, what would it be? Underline one of the options to indicate what you'd *like* your child to do.

Then ask yourself: What would your child *actually* do? Circle one of the options to indicate your prediction.

Finally, think about this: In each case, how could you make your chosen ending more likely? What can you do in the next six months to help your child learn and practice that kind of self-discipline?

Story 1: Let Them Eat Cake

This afternoon you baked and frosted a chocolate cake for the Bible study group that's coming over tonight. It's your child's favorite kind of cake, but you've told him or her not to eat any of it. Unfortunately, you don't happen to have any other snacks in the house right now—unless you count the gummy worms from last Halloween, which have turned hard as concrete. Your child claims to be starving. But you can't guard the cake; you have to spend the time between now and the Bible study shoveling snow off the driveway so that your guests won't fall down and sue you.

Choose your own ending:

  a. Your child has the self-discipline to ignore the cake and go on a fast in solidarity with hungry kids who would be glad to have the gummy worms.

  b. Your child exercises enough self-discipline to hollow out the cake from underneath, leaving an empty shell for the Bible study group.

c. Your child eats the entire cake, but has the self-discipline to leave the gummy worms for your guests.
   d. other _____

Story 2: The Manhattan Project
It's Monday, and Friday is approaching like doomsday. That's the deadline for your child to bring his or her science project to school. Your child has wasted the last month flip-flopping between doing a project about batteries made from potatoes or one about the motivational speaking skills of parrots. "I'll get it done," your child keeps saying, but all you're seeing is a lot of text messages being sent to friends and precious few potatoes or parrots. The science project will determine whether your child gets a B or a D in the class, and could drag his or her overall grade average into the basement.

Choose your own ending:
   a. Your child has the self-discipline to stop text-messaging, watching TV, and sleeping long enough to spend his or her own allowance on a potato, a bunch of wires, and 64 square feet of poster board—and finish the project by Wednesday night.
   b. Your child exercises enough self-discipline to choose an easier project ("Do Round Waffles Float Longer Than Square Ones?") and get it done by sunset on Thursday.
   c. Your child has the self-discipline to fake illness on Friday, thereby gaining the weekend on which to procrastinate further.
   d. other _____

Story 3: Cash for Clunkers
Your child's birthday was two weeks ago; he or she got an unusually generous $100 check from Grandma. You can think of all kinds of things that $100 could buy. Your child can think of only one: a pair of designer sunglasses available on an Internet auction site. You're certain that a year from now those shades will be gathering dust next to the ancient

Pokemon cards in your child's room. And the peers your kid wants to impress won't even remember how "hot" those glasses were. But your child *has* to have them, it seems, or the space-time continuum will unravel.

Choose your own ending:

a. Your child exercises enough self-discipline to wait two days before bidding on the sunglasses, in order to check prices on other Web sites—but still insists on making the purchase.

b. Your child, realizing that he or she could have something much more valuable by tithing the money and investing the rest, has the self-discipline to postpone gratification indefinitely.

c. Your child, learning that the sunglasses are available locally, has the self-discipline to wait five minutes before demanding to be driven to the mall.

d. other _____

BRINGING IT HOME

Insight for Your Week

Some suggestions about chores and discipline:

- If a job is not done diligently, have your child practice doing it. She'll learn to be more thorough if she's made to sweep the floor three or four times because her first effort wasn't good enough.
- If your children whine or argue when you dole out their chores, add another to each list. Once they hit extra chore number three, they'll get the point and stop complaining when they're asked to help out.
- Do you have to constantly remind your child to feed his pet? Mount a little box on top of the pet's house or cage and put your child's lunch money or lunch bag in it. If he wants his lunch that day, he must make sure his pet gets its lunch first.

- Whenever my brother Casey forgets to take out the trash the night before the garbage truck comes, my mother sneaks into his room and sets his alarm for 5:30 in the morning.

This gives him time to wake up and carry the can out to the curb. (This correction can work well for any job that is supposed to be done before going to bed.)

- Have you ever considered charging a 10-cent reminder fee when your child forgets a chore? Let's face it, a child who has been told since day one to set the dinner table is not really "forgetting" to do it. I require my children to keep a couple of their dollars in dimes in a jar. This way, it's much simpler to collect the fee for their "forgetfulness."
- Is it your child's job to take out the trash or the recyclables? Doth the can runneth over? If so, simply take out the trash for him . . . but leave the can in the middle of his bedroom floor. He may be more prone to take it out as the stench rises.
- If your child's responsibility is loading the dishwasher, and the prerinsing job never gets done thoroughly, explain to her, "If the dishes aren't clean, you must wash them again—by hand."
- I have a friend whose son's morning chore was to get the pooper-scooper and clean up the doggie gifts littering the backyard. The boy was not doing this job with much diligence, so his father came up with this creative solution: After the boy had completed the task, he would be required to run through the yard barefoot! From then on, their lawn was perfectly clean.
- You can really get your child's attention by ordering her to do meaningless chores, such as moving the woodpile to the other side of the yard or digging a large hole and then filling it up again.
- The next time your child does not do a diligent job of scrubbing the dinner dishes, rinsing the spinach leaves, or wiping the table, insist that she go back and re-do everyone else's dishes, spinach

leaves, or place at the table. But the less-than-spectacular job she did should be good enough for her things.

- I like the creative correction I received from a mom of three boys. One Saturday morning she gave them a list of chores to have done by noon. At eleven o'clock they were still in their pajamas, watching cartoons, and hadn't even started on the chores. She didn't nag; she simply waited until the stroke of noon. Then she called a neighbor who had children the same ages as hers and offered to pay them to come over and do those chores. The neighbor kids jumped at the chance, rushed right over, and quickly worked through the list. When they were done, the neighbor kids were allowed to go into the boys' rooms and choose any toy they wanted in payment. Another idea would have been to pay with the boys' allowance for the week.
- If your kids have assigned chores and they ask you to do something special, simply respond with, "Did you wash the dishes?" or "Is your bed made?" or whatever chores should be accomplished by then. Whether they answer with "yes" or "no," you then respond with, "That's the answer to your question." Soon they will get the message not to ask you for anything special unless they have all their chores done first.

—Lisa Whelchel[10]

Chapter 6

PREPARING YOUR HEART TO PARENT

A pair of Christian parents seemed unaware that they were destroying one of their daughters by verbally abusing her.

"You're too fat," they'd tell her one day.

"You're too skinny," they'd tell her the next.

Then it was, "You're so stupid you'll never be a success at what you want to do."

When it became clear that the girl had become suicidal, the parents claimed to be mystified. Opening wide, innocent eyes, they told their friends at church, "We have no idea what's wrong with her. She's just moody."

Behind the doors of other Christian homes, other awful secrets have been kept. One girl opted out of "being good" when her pastor father was arrested for drug possession and use. Another slid downhill when her stepfather abused her. A young man couldn't deal with his father's pornography habit. And no one on the outside had any idea what was happening.

Can you open up your doors and let the truth step out? You might want to pray about that. Ask God to show you the truth and set you free (John 8:32). Like training, truth often hurts—but it's the only way to the winner's circle.

—Joe White with Lissa Halls Johnson[11]

FINDING YOURSELF

Identifying Your Needs

Take a couple of minutes to fill out the following survey.

1. You prepared for your relationship with your child by
   ___ reading *What to Expect When You're Expecting*.
   ___ working on your relationship with God.
   ___ hitting yourself over the head repeatedly with a hammer.
   ___ other _____

2. Which of the following song titles best describes your relationship with God?
   ___ "Strangers in the Night"
   ___ "Close to You"
   ___ "Just My Imagination"
   ___ other _____

3. How is your relationship with God like your child's relationship with you?
   ___ Your child looks to you for direction and protection.
   ___ Your child receives love and forgiveness from you.
   ___ Your child thinks you're rich and invisible.
   ___ other _____

4. If you treated your child the way God treats you,
   ___ you'd be named Parent of the Year.
   ___ you'd be arrested for neglect.
   ___ you'd have to increase your child's allowance substantially.
   ___ other _____

5. The biggest improvement you could make in your relationship with God is
   ___ spending more time with Him.
   ___ learning from His affirmation and discipline.
   ___ speaking only Greek and Hebrew.
   ___ other _____

6. You hope that someday your child will describe your relationship as follows:
   ___ "No parent and child were ever closer."
   ___ "He [or she] taught me everything I know."
   ___ "I was raised by wolves."
   ___ other _____

CATCHING THE VISION

Watching and Discussing the DVD

While we're parenting, who's parenting us? God is, and He's doing it perfectly. We could all learn something from His example.

In this DVD segment, Gary Thomas and Dr. Juli Slattery team up to make the connection between God's parenting and ours. Through the way He "raises" us, God wants to teach us about love, sacrifice, and forgiveness.

You might call this "parallel parenting." It starts when we begin a relationship with God. It deepens as we let Him bring us up His way, and as we invite Him to help us grow as both parents and children.

After viewing the DVD, use questions like these to help you think through what you saw and heard.

1. When did you first feel "grown up" enough to be a parent? Did you still have more growing to do? Is God "finished with you yet"?

2. Which of the following have you learned the most about by being a parent?
    - love
    - sacrifice
    - forgiveness
    - disgusting bodily functions
    - other _____

3. What would your parents recognize in the way you raise your kids? Would they be proud of the influence they've had, or regretful? Why?

4. Do you agree with the following statements? If so, how do they affect the way you parent? If not, how would you rephrase them to reflect your opinion?
    - Family life is a laboratory for building holiness.
    - We either become miserable or we grow to become more like Christ.
    - The closer we get to Christ, the more our kids will pursue Him as well.
    - I can't imagine raising my kids without God; the fear would overwhelm me.

5. What's one trait you hope your kids gain from you? What have you done to encourage that? What's one trait God wants you to pick up from Him? What has He done to encourage that?

6. When you hear people say that God "parents" you, what's your reaction?
    - "What kind of parent is invisible and never says anything?"

- "He's always been there for me."
- "I'm glad He's not like my earthly parents."
- "I must be missing something."
- other _____

7. Which of the following is most like the atmosphere in which you grew up? If the parenting style in your family was a problem, how would you like yours to be different?
    - a reality TV show
    - a Norman Rockwell painting
    - a freezer
    - a concentration camp

8. What is hardest for you about working on your relationship with God? Which of the following is the biggest obstacle?
    - I doubt that God really wants a close relationship with me.
    - I can't find the time.
    - My family keeps interrupting me.
    - My job and kids take all my energy.
    - other _____

DIGGING DEEPER

Bible Study

> "I am the good shepherd; I know my sheep and my sheep know me—just as the Father knows me and I know the Father—and I lay down my life for the sheep." (John 10:14-15)

1. How do you feel about relating to Jesus as sheep relate to a shepherd? Which of the following comes closest to your reaction?
    ___ "I don't know a thing about sheep, so I can't say."

___ "Sheep are stupid, aren't they? I'm not sure I like the comparison."

___ "I feel more secure knowing that Jesus wants to protect me as a shepherd protects his flock."

___ other _ _____

2. On a scale of 1 to 10 (10 highest), how are you doing at each of the following "sheep specialties"?

___ knowing your shepherd

___ following your shepherd

___ trusting your shepherd to guard you and your family

"I am the true vine, and my Father is the gardener. He cuts off every branch in me that bears no fruit, while every branch that does bear fruit he prunes so that it will be even more fruitful. You are already clean because of the word I have spoken to you. Remain in me, and I will remain in you. No branch can bear fruit by itself; it must remain in the vine. Neither can you bear fruit unless you remain in me.

"I am the vine; you are the branches. If a man remains in me and I in him, he will bear much fruit; apart from me you can do nothing. If anyone does not remain in me, he is like a branch that is thrown away and withers; such branches are picked up, thrown into the fire and burned. If you remain in me and my words remain in you, ask whatever you wish, and it will be given you. This is to my Father's glory, that you bear much fruit, showing yourselves to be my disciples.

"As the Father has loved me, so have I loved you. Now remain in my love. If you obey my commands, you will remain in my love, just as I have obeyed my Father's commands and remain in his love. I have told you this so that my joy may be in you and that your joy may be complete. My command is this: Love each other as I have loved you. Greater love has no one than this, that he lay down his life for his friends. You are my

friends if you do what I command. I no longer call you servants, because a servant does not know his master's business. Instead, I have called you friends, for everything that I learned from my Father I have made known to you. You did not choose me, but I chose you and appointed you to go and bear fruit—fruit that will last. Then the Father will give you whatever you ask in my name. This is my command: Love each other."
(John 15:1-17)

3. If you want to prepare for a right relationship with your child by strengthening your relationship with God, which three of the following will be your top priority? Why?

   ___ "remaining" in Christ
   ___ remembering that without Jesus, you can do nothing
   ___ bearing fruit
   ___ asking for whatever you need
   ___ obeying Jesus' commands
   ___ loving each other
   ___ seeing yourself as a friend of Jesus
   ___ other _____

4. How is the relationship Christ wants with you like the relationship you want with your child? How is it different?

5. What kind of "fruit" could a strong relationship with God produce in the following situations? What might stand in the way of producing that fruit?

   ___ You're frustrated because the basketball coach is keeping your child on the bench.
   ___ Your 7-year-old can't seem to stop wetting the bed.
   ___ Your 11-year-old stepson won't accept your ban on video games that depict shooting people.

66 THE POWER OF LOVE

MAKING IT WORK
Applying the Principles

THE SPIRITUAL FOOD PYRAMID

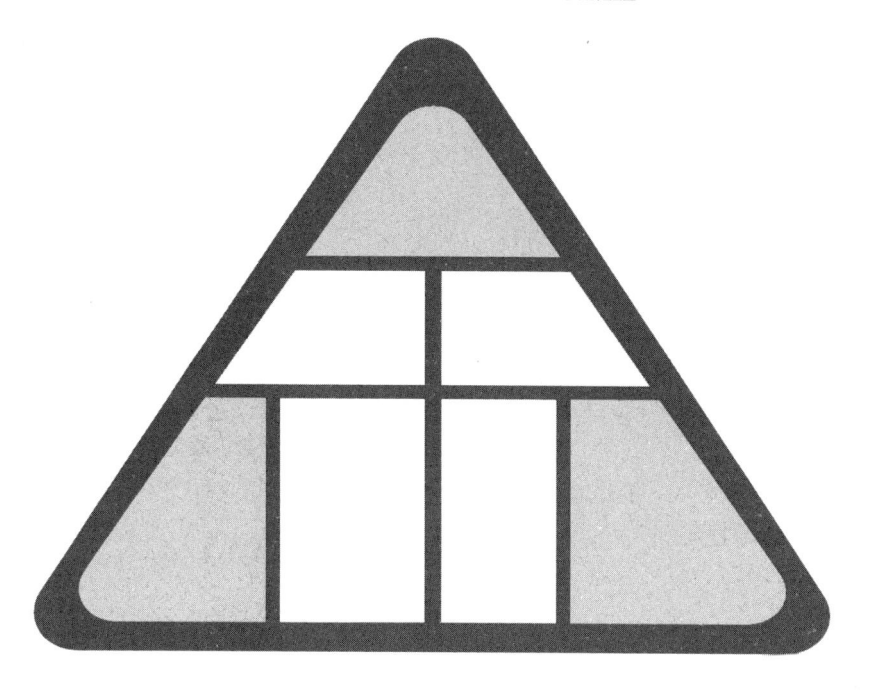

NUTRIENT LIST

PRAYING WITH YOUR CHILD
PRAYING ON YOUR OWN
BIBLE READING ON YOUR OWN
BELONGING TO A BIBLE STUDY GROUP
BEING ACCOUNTABLE TO A CHRISTIAN FRIEND
SERVING OTHERS WITH YOUR CHILD
SERVING OTHERS AS PART OF A GROUP
LISTENING TO PRAISE CHORUSES
LISTENING TO HYMNS

LISTENING TO CHRISTIAN RADIO
LISTENING TO SERMONS
WORSHIPING ON YOUR OWN
WORSHIPING WITH A GROUP
WATCHING CHRISTIAN TV AND MOVIES WITH YOUR CHILD
READING CHRISTIAN BOOKS AND MAGAZINES
READING CHRISTIAN BOOKS WITH OR TO YOUR CHILD
SURFING CHRISTIAN WEB SITES WITH YOUR CHILD
SURFING CHRISTIAN WEB SITES ON YOUR OWN
MEMORIZING SCRIPTURE WITH YOUR CHILD
MEMORIZING SCRIPTURE ON YOUR OWN

Choose the seven "nutrients" from the list that you think could help you grow most in your relationship with God and with your child. Write them on the Spiritual Food Pyramid in the spaces provided; the ingredient you think is most important should go in the top space, with placement of the others showing the value you think they have. Then ask yourself: Does your schedule during a typical week reflect your version of the pyramid? Why or why not?

BRINGING IT HOME

Insight for Your Week

It was a toddler rite-of-passage night in our home. After sleeping for her first year in a cradle in the master bedroom walk-in closet, Clancy was graduating to a real crib. Meanwhile, Tucker was parking his car-shaped bed by the curb in exchange for bunk beds, and Haven was relinquishing the baby bed for the bottom bunk.

Haven was nervous about the switch to a big-girl bed. She crawled, wide-eyed, into her new bottom bunk and lay there stiffly, clutching her "geekie" (blanket), sucking on her "bappy" (pacifier), while cuddling her "Barney" (dinosaur). She fixed her gaze on the bottom of the top bunk, as if she were afraid to even look around the room.

Tucker was anxious, too, but he was also excited. Wired and hopping around the room, he couldn't wait to try out his new bed. When it actually came to crawling up to the top bunk, however, he hesitated. Tucker had suddenly "forgotten" how to climb a ladder. After several minutes of coaxing, we finally got him into bed, but the challenge didn't end there. Within 15 minutes, he had bumped his head on the ceiling, trying to stand up; caught his arm in the rail, trying to lean over and talk to Haven; and gotten his foot stuck between the wall and the bed, trying to turn the light switch on with his toe.

None of us was getting much sleep—and after enduring half an hour of Tucker's noisy mischief, Steve had had enough. He scrambled out of bed and stormed into the children's room.

"If you kids don't settle down," he ordered, "you will sleep in your old beds!" To drive home his point, Steve stood for a moment, gazing at Tucker and Haven. His hands were held up in exasperation, and he was clothed in nothing but his briefs.

Tucker obviously couldn't get past the figure of Steve standing half-clothed in the shadows. "Dad," he commented, "you look like you're about to die on a cross like Jesus!"

Suppressing a chuckle, Steve gave up and went back to bed.

Tucker's comment made us all laugh, but it reveals a nugget of truth: Our children closely identify us with God. We as parents represent Him to our kids. As they observe us each day, they create a picture of Him in their minds and hearts. They may paint an angry tyrant, waiting to pounce on their tiniest mistake, or they may sketch a God so little and far removed as to barely exist. Sadly, some children even draw God to be their own size.

Given that our children learn to relate to God through our example, we must take seriously our job of parenting. God has blessed us with this role; I believe it's our primary purpose as parents. But how can we represent Him to our kids and do it in a healthy way? How can we help them to understand that obeying us—in love—is directly related to loving and obeying their heavenly Father?

Modeling God to our kids is a tall order. In fact, I would be the first to admit that my representation of God is imperfect. But that's the nature of a reflection. It's backward in a mirror, upside-down in a spoon, blurry in a window, and always one-dimensional. Though we should strive to be godly, we can never perfectly reflect God. Instead, our goal should be to ensure that our reflection of God draws our children closer to Him—and that it makes them long to touch the real thing.

—Lisa Whelchel[12]

NOTES

1. Adapted from Dr. Kevin Leman, *Home Court Advantage* (Wheaton, Ill.: Focus on the Family/Tyndale House Publishers, 2005), pp. 29-30.
2. Adapted from Joe White with Lissa Halls Johnson, *Sticking with Your Teen* (Carol Stream, Ill.: Focus on the Family/Tyndale House Publishers, 2006), pp. 17-18.
3. Adapted from Tim Sanford, *Losing Control and Liking It* (Carol Stream, Ill.: Focus on the Family/Tyndale House Publishers, 2009), pp. 21-23.
4. White with Johnson, pp. 80-82.
5. Sanford, pp. 25-27.
6. White with Johnson, pp. 82-86.
7. Leman, pp. 191-192.
8. Adapted from Lisa Whelchel, *Creative Correction* (Wheaton, Ill.: Focus on the Family/Tyndale House Publishers, 2005), pp. 58-59, 61-63.
9. Ibid., pp. 175-176.
10. Ibid., pp. 158-161.
11. White with Johnson, pp. 24-25.
12. Whelchel, pp. 17-18, 20.

About Our DVD Presenters

Essentials of Parenting: The Power of Love

Carey Casey is chief executive officer of the National Center for Fathering and fathers.com. Driven by his faith and the example of his own father, Carey passionately encourages men to live out a lifelong commitment to loving, coaching, and modeling for their children, encouraging the fatherless, and enlisting other men to join a movement to change the fathering culture in America. He is the author of *Championship Fathering: How to Win at Being a Dad.* Carey has been married to his wife, Melanie, for over thirty years; they have four children and five grandchildren.

Gary Thomas is a writer and the founder/director of the Center for Evangelical Spirituality, a speaking and writing ministry that combines Scripture, history, and the Christian classics. His books include *Sacred Marriage, Authentic Faith* (winner of the Gold Medallion award in 2003), and *Seeking the Face of God.* Gary has spoken in 49 states and four countries and has served as the campus pastor at Western Seminary, where he is an adjunct professor. Gary, his wife, Lisa, and their three kids live in Bellingham, Washington.

Dr. Julianna Slattery is a family psychologist and broadcast host for Focus on the Family. Juli is the author of *Finding the Hero in Your Husband, Guilt-Free Motherhood,* and *Beyond the Masquerade.* Applying biblical wisdom to the everyday lives of women and families is her passion. She shares her message with a combination of humor, candor, and foundational truth. Juli earned a doctor of psychology and master of science in clinical psychology at Florida Institute of Technology, a master of arts in psychology from Biola University, and a bachelor of arts from Wheaton

College. Juli and her husband, Mike, live in Colorado Springs and are the parents of three boys.

Dr. Bob Barnes is president of Sheridan House Family Ministries in Fort Lauderdale, Florida. He presents seminars and conferences on parenting and marriage throughout North America, hosts a weekly radio program, and is the author of several books for families—including *Ready for Responsibility: How to Equip Your Children for Work and Marriage* and *Raising Confident Kids*. Bob has been married to Rosemary Johnson Barnes since 1972. They have two children, Torrey and Robey.

Julie Barnhill is the author of several books including *Every Mother Deserves a Good Laugh; Motherhood: The Guilt That Keeps on Giving;* and *She's Gonna Blow! Real Help for Moms Dealing with Anger*. She has appeared on Oprah and other TV and radio programs, and speaks to groups frequently on the subject of motherhood. Julie and her husband have three children.

FOCUS ON THE FAMILY®

Welcome to the Family

Whether you purchased this book, borrowed it or received it as a gift, we're glad you're reading it. It's just one of the many helpful, encouraging and biblically based resources produced by Focus on the Family® for people in all stages of life.

Focus began in 1977 with the vision of one man, Dr. James Dobson, a licensed psychologist and author of numerous best-selling books on marriage, parenting and family. Alarmed by the societal, political and economic pressures that were threatening the existence of the American family, Dr. Dobson founded Focus on the Family with one employee and a once-a-week radio broadcast aired on 36 stations.

Now an international organization reaching millions of people daily, Focus on the Family is dedicated to preserving values and strengthening and encouraging families through the life-changing message of Jesus Christ.

Focus on the Family MAGAZINES

These faith-building, character-developing publications address the interests, issues, concerns, and challenges faced by every member of your family from preschool through the senior years.

For More INFORMATION

ONLINE:
Log on to
FocusOnTheFamily.com
In Canada, log on to
FocusOnTheFamily.ca

PHONE:
Call toll-free:
**800-A-FAMILY
(232-6459)**
In Canada, call toll-free:
800-661-9800

THRIVING FAMILY™
Marriage & Parenting

FOCUS ON THE FAMILY CLUBHOUSE JR.®
Ages 4 to 8

FOCUS ON THE FAMILY CLUBHOUSE®
Ages 8 to 12

FOCUS ON THE FAMILY CITIZEN®
U.S. news issues

Rev. 4/10

ESSENTIALS OF PARENTING™
Resources from Focus on the Family®

In *Essentials of Parenting™: Raising Kids with a Faith that Lasts*, authorities like Dr. Tim Kimmel, Mark Holmen, and Larry Fowler introduce you to one of your greatest privileges—helping your child begin a relationship with God. Includes a six-session DVD and a Resource CD-ROM with Leader's Guide, Participant's Guide, Campaign Planning Guide, and print-ready promotional materials.*

In *Essentials of Parenting™: The Power of Love*, experts like Carey Casey, Gary Thomas, and Dr. Juli Slattery show how to enrich and enjoy the bond between your child and yourself. Includes a six-session DVD and a Resource CD-ROM with Leader's Guide, Participant's Guide, Campaign Planning Guide, and print-ready promotional materials.*

In *Essentials of Parenting™: Be Prepared*, mentors like Dannah Gresh, Dr. Bob Barnes, and Dr. Juli Slattery present practical plans for dealing with dangers, including Internet porn, alcohol, drugs, eating disorders, and premarital sex. Includes a seven-session DVD and a Resource CD-ROM with Leader's Guide, Participant's Guide, Campaign Planning Guide, and print-ready promotional materials.*

*Printed Participant's Guides also available for purchase at FocusOnTheFamily.com/resources

FOCUS ON THE FAMILY
FocusOnTheFamily.com

For more information log on to FocusOnTheFamily.com/Resources or call toll-free: 800-A-FAMILY

In Canada, log on to FocusOnTheFamily.ca or call toll-free: 800-661-9800

CP0426